THE UGH FACTOR

FACTOR

Julia Golding

Illustrated by Euan Cook

Chapter 1
Star Makers

How had it come to this? Leo waited in the wings, knowing that he and his bandmates were about to kill their reputation as the coolest kids in their school. Their image would die a gruesome death before an audience of millions.

'And now we come to our last act of the evening,' boomed the voice in the cavernous auditorium.

Lights danced and flashed on-stage, ratcheting up the tension. 'They are the youngest performers to get this far on any series of *Star Makers*, so make them feel welcome!'

'Please let a meteor strike right now,' groaned Leo. His sister, Anji, looked grim; his best mates, Dan and Tris, tense.

'Are we really gonna do this?' asked Tris.

Dan swallowed. 'We can't back out now, guys. It's too late.'

'I give you,' bellowed the announcer over the screams and whistles, 'The Cutie Pies and their faithful hound, Bows!'

Leo had a split second to register the stunned look on the familiar faces in the front row as he ran on-stage. Like flicking the first domino in a line leading to a big red 'danger' button, the band had set off this disaster and now could do nothing to stop it.

And it had all begun so innocently …

A month ago …

'Pass the cereal, Leo,' said Anji.

Leo slid the box along the breakfast bar. He hated mornings. His brain was still asleep. Only his body was present and that was under protest.

'Hey, Zombie-boy, milk! I'm getting old here.' Anji pointed to the carton on the far side of him, her collection of silver bracelets jingling brightly.

Why did he get a younger sister who was always so upbeat in the morning? Time for some Zombie-boy revenge. Leo picked up the carton and lurched to stand behind her.

'Me gonna eat your brains.' He put the cold milk carton on her bare neck.

'Leo!' Anji jumped up from her stool, her beaded braids clacking as she dodged the milk. 'I hate it when you do that!'

'Feed me! Feed me!' growled Leo, shuffle-chasing her around the counter.

'Stop it!' Anji began to giggle. 'You are so evil!'

Leo sniffed the air. 'Uh? What's this? She no good zombie food. She have no brains.'

Anji grabbed the milk from him. 'Then that "no brains" thing must run in the family.'

Grinning at each other, with points scored about even, they went back to their breakfast. Mum came in, dressed in her blue nurse's uniform. Her straightened black hair was held back by a clip in the shape of a guitar, a present from Leo and Anji last birthday. The local TV newsreader prattled away on the screen over Mum's head as she made coffee. Extreme weather. Wars. Financial problems. Same news as always.

But then the picture exploded in a shower of stars and a familiar theme tune came on.

'My favourite show!' Mum hummed along to the song for *Star Makers*. Anji put down her spoon.

The newsreader fixed all three of them in his twinkling gaze. 'And finally, fame and fortune is coming to our region.'

'As if,' said Anji. 'Nothing ever happens here.'

'Ssh!' said Mum. 'I want to hear this.'

'Do you have star power?' asked the newsreader. 'If the answer to that is "Yes!" the team at *Star Makers* want you. They are holding open auditions in the city leisure centre this Saturday.'

Uh-oh. Leo could guess what was going to happen next. Mum had dropped hints before that she thought he and Anji were destined for great things in the music business. Her predictions had started when he had put together a band with his mates, Tris and Dan. Anji had joined them six months ago and they were going from strength to strength.

He slid down from his seat and tried to escape, but his mother was too quick.

'Oh Leo, Anji, this is wonderful!'

Anji scowled. 'No, it really isn't. It's a terrible programme. They always pick such lame winners.'

Anji's taste in music was whatever everyone else hated. In her opinion, a real rock star had to dress in goth black and look like they'd been recently exhumed from their grave and forced to sing about being miserable. Despite this weakness, she was a great singer and played guitar so the band couldn't do without her.

'How can you say that? Last year's winner has been at number one for a month with 'Ooh, ooh, I love you'.' Mum looked hurt by Anji's scorn.

Anji shuddered delicately. 'Exactly.'

'But you're both so talented. Your group played so well together at the school concert. This is your big chance. I just know it.' Mum smiled at them both in that doting way perfected by mothers over the ages: slightly mad and very determined.

Leo sensed their doom closing in.

'But our sound is indie, not pop,' he said. 'We're

just not the kind of band *Star Makers* likes.'

'In fact, nobody likes us yet,' Anji muttered, 'and that's how *I* like it.'

Leo thought his sister took being alternative a bit far. As the frontman and main vocalist, he hoped they'd slowly gather a following from those who liked good music, and maybe even a recording contract one day. *Star Makers* was totally not the right route as the programme promoted the mainstream and the shallow.

Mum folded her arms across her chest. 'Of course they'll like you! And you have to start somewhere in the business.'

'This is a contest for pop singers,' repeated Leo.

'And your point is? It's all singing, isn't it?'

Mum just didn't get it. Leo looked at Anji, hoping she would have a good excuse. She doubled over and coughed.

'Oh no. I think … ' (cough) 'I'm ill … ' (cough). 'Seriously ill.'

'Really, darling?' Mum tapped her foot. 'What a shame. Because I was thinking I'd buy you both tickets to Glastonbury if you went to the audition.

I noticed that your favourite bands are in the line-up this year.'

Anji stopped coughing. 'You mean you've finally agreed we can go to a music festival?'

'For the whole weekend?' asked Leo. This was brilliant! Until now, Mum had avoided Glastonbury and other festivals like a vampire does garlic, convinced that her kids were too young.

Mum nodded. 'Tris' dad talked me into it last night and he has promised to keep an eye on you. But if you're likely to fall ill so suddenly, Anji, then sadly I'll have to cancel our plans as it wouldn't be fair to expect him to look after you.'

'I feel a lot better, Mum.' Anji exchanged a glance with Leo. 'In fact, I think I'm over whatever it was. Completely.'

'You'll do the audition?' Mum smiled.

'Yes,' said Anji.

'Promise?'

'We promise,' said Leo. Both of them would walk barefoot over burning coals, let alone go to a stupid audition, to get to Glastonbury. 'I mean, how bad can it be?' he added to Anji under his breath.

Leo convened an emergency meeting of their band at lunchtime on the school playing field.

'Here's the thing, guys,' said Leo, scuffing the leaves. 'Our mum's said we can go to Glastonbury.'

'That's good, isn't it?' asked Dan, perched on the parallel bars of the outdoor gym. The tallest boy in the year, his trouser legs were always a little too short for him, as he outgrew them like a runner bean shooting up its pole. He played bass guitar and had a nice voice if he could be coaxed out of his shyness to sing. 'Why do you look so upset about it?'

'There's a hitch.'

Tris, their drummer, groaned. 'Here we go.' He slapped his hand to his forehead. 'Take cover, Dan. I know what he's going to say.'

Leo was taken aback. 'You do?'

'I watched TV this morning too.' Tris pulled his hood up over his crop of dark blond hair and curled his bony knees up to his chest. 'And I know your mum. I don't want to hear.' He screwed his eyes shut, falling into his role as the band's very own prophet of doom.

Anji bopped him lightly on the head with her bag

to get his attention. 'Tris, you've got to help us!'

'Hey, guys, will one of you tell me what's happening?' asked Dan.

'It's our mum. She made us promise to enter our band for the *Star Makers* audition.' Leo pulled a face.

'You're joking?' Dan hooted with laughter. 'You always said you'd rather dance in a pink glitter suit in front of our whole year group than go in for that competition.'

'Yeah, well, I had a change of heart.'

'He's been bribed,' said Tris from the depths of his hood.

'You're serious?' Dan looked like he had just swallowed a cockroach.

'I'm afraid so.'

'You can't do this to me – to us! Where's this leading? Loserville, that's where.'

'With no way back,' added Tris.

'Aw, come on, guys!' Anji tried her sad face on them, big brown eyes just on the verge of tears. 'Dan, you said just last week that going to Glastonbury would be no fun without us.'

Dan hated it when Anji got upset. He held out

a hand to her. 'Anji, it's not that we don't want to help you.'

'So, what's the problem then?'

'It's just ... No, no, not the puppy eyes! You know I can't argue when you do that!' He ran his fingers through his brown hair, making it spike in wild tufts.

'Give in, Dan,' growled Tris. 'You know you're going to.'

'All right, Anji. I'll do it. Tris will too.'

'You'll have to tie me in a sack to get me there,' muttered Tris darkly.

'I will if necessary,' replied Dan. 'Anji and Leo need us.'

'I'll help carry him,' said Leo, amused by Tris' horror-struck expression. 'I'll take his head, you take the legs.'

'I'm not being carried like Cleopatra in a carpet through the city centre to be unrolled on-stage at *Star Makers*!' spluttered Tris.

'That's settled then. Tris will walk in on his own legs,' Leo said with a grin.

Once Dan had decided he had to do something for Anji's sake, Leo knew they were home and dry.

'Just the audition – no more,' warned Tris.

Dan brushed a hand over Anji's shoulder – not quite a hug but almost. 'But no one at school is to hear about it. I don't know about you Year 7s, Anji, but the other boys in Year 8 will never let us forget it if they find out we entered.'

'Dan, you're the best!' Anji rewarded him with a huge smile.

'I just hope the judges don't think that. Auditions only, then we end this,' said Tris firmly.

'It's not like there's any chance we're what they're looking for,' Leo frowned. 'Is there?' Their band was getting good; recently, things had gelled and Leo thought they might be really going somewhere. 'Guys, we need a plan to make sure we lose.'

Chapter 2
How to lose a competition

They had agreed that they would all come to band practice that night with their ideas. They met at Tris' house as he had a soundproof basement for his drum kit. His dad was an old rocker who had played for the band Dead Heads until settling down to be an accountant. Knowing the dynamics of a band, he provided snacks and let them get on with it – just how they liked it.

'OK, what are we going to sing?' asked Dan. He leafed through their songs. 'If we put Tris on as lead, we'll definitely lose.'

Tris threw a handful of popcorn at him.

'Just a suggestion.' Dan grinned.

Tris' dog, Bones, got off his bed to vacuum up the popcorn. Bones was so ugly he was almost cute, a big black patch over his left eye and a stubby tail that beat to and fro like a windscreen wiper on fast.

'I had an idea on the way over.' Anji dropped down on the beanbag and scratched Bones' neck.

'Go on.' Dan sat beside her.

'I think we should be everything we hate.'

'I hate your music and we are not singing any of that dull stuff,' grumbled Leo.

'My music is awesome!'

Tris stepped in before the brother and sister returned to an old dispute. 'Go on, Anji, tell us what you mean.'

'I wasn't talking about my *wonderful* sort of music,' she glared at Leo, 'but about things we all think are rubbish, things that have the "ugh!" factor. Let's make a list.'

'OK. Good idea.' Dan grabbed a pad of paper and a pen. 'I hate pink.' He wrote PINK in big letters.

'I hate pictures of fluffy kittens,' said Tris. Bones looked up and growled.

FLUFFY KITTENS, wrote Dan.

'Love, hearts and flowers – all of those go on the list,' said Leo.

Dan chewed the end of his pen. 'Good start. Anji, this was your idea: what do you want to put on here?'

Anji tugged the end of one of her braids. 'I can't stand rainbows and unicorns.'

'What? I thought you loved them!' said Dan. 'I've been buying you birthday cards with unicorns on since, like, forever! I spend months hunting them down.'

'I know. I didn't want to say.'

Dan looked crestfallen.

'I did like them, Dan, when I was six.' Anji shrugged. 'People decided it was my thing and now I can't move in my bedroom without coming across cushions, duvet covers and posters I've tried to hide.'

'I'm sorry.' Dan had been trying so hard to impress Anji since he had woken up to the fact that she wasn't just Leo's baby sister.

'Don't be sorry. It's good to finally be able to admit it.'

'OK then. Next birthday I'm getting you a card with a skull and a Rottweiler on it.'

'Looking forward to it.'

'*Meanwhile*,' said Leo, breaking into the heavy eye contact moment between the pair of them, 'Anji's extra stuff can be made into costumes.'

'Finally, a use for them!' Anji smiled at Dan. 'Cool.'

'And I have these gruesome jumpers knitted by my gran,' admitted Dan.

'What do they look like?' Leo wasn't sure any knitwear could be bad enough to fit in with this idea.

'Grim. She only knits in pink wool and seems to think I like big flowers.' The others laughed. 'Yeah, I know. I think she takes her style notes from the Scooby Doo Mystery Machine.'

'Cool! I mean *not* cool!' Leo rubbed his hands together. 'Jumpers sorted. We can ask Mum to make us trousers out of Anji's old curtains.'

'She'll insist on making me a skirt,' complained Anji.

'That's the price for her help.' Leo shrugged. He was struggling with the idea of wearing a pink flowered sweater and unicorn trousers, so found her grumbles silly. At least she was a girl and wouldn't have to go into exile if anyone found out. 'We'll tell no one from school that we're entering and disguise ourselves in case any images get posted online – make our hair dorky.' He thought longingly of his black jeans and T-shirt that he wore when fronting the band. He had had his hair shaved in swirls; he'd have to cover that up or it would wreck the image.

Tris went over to his drum kit and began tapping out a rhythm. 'So who's going to write the song?'

Leo was their main lyricist. 'I'll do it.'

'I'll help,' offered Anji.

'I've got a melody that might work,' admitted Dan, their composer.

'Better get down to it then,' said Tris.

Leo took a fresh sheet of paper off the pad. 'Don't worry – I'll write such a dumb song, no one in their right mind will vote for us.'

Chapter 3
Best laid plans . . .

It was far worse than Leo had thought. Half the town had turned up for the auditions and the queue snaked right round the block. There would inevitably be someone in there that knew them. He slipped on his sunglasses and pulled his bobble hat down to his ears.

'How much do you want to go to Glastonbury again?' asked Dan, looking about him in hope of a getaway car.

'Desperately,' said Anji firmly, linking her arm to his. Dan smiled down at her, forgetting he wanted to make a run for it. Anji checked the time on her phone. 'Where's Tris?'

'If he's got any sense, he's bottled out.' Dan shifted the bulging bag of sweaters to the other hand.

'Hi, guys.' Tris approached from behind, Bones on a lead.

'What have you done to him?' asked Leo. The dog was wearing a big pink bow around his black studded collar and looked bewildered. From Bones' point of view, his owner had suddenly gone crazy.

'I decided if I was going to face total humiliation, he could too.'

Anji crouched beside the dog and gave his neck a scratch. 'Aw, Bones, you look kind of cute, you know, in a really weird way.'

The dog licked her cheek.

The line shuffled forward.

'Learned the words?' Tris asked Leo.

'Sadly they are burned on my brain for all eternity.'

'They're so lame, I wouldn't be surprised if they boo us offstage.' Anji danced nervously in the line as they edged forward.

Once inside the leisure centre, they gave their names to the lady on the door and were ushered into the waiting area. Around them, local groups were warming up. The Slicers were running through their dark, edgy number about life on the streets; the girl band, The Sugarlumps, practised their dance steps.

'Do we need a routine?' asked Dan. 'You know, put the cherry on top of the lame cake?'

'How about this?' Anji, the best dancer among them, did a few steps and made a heart shape against her chest with her thumbs and fingers.

Leo nodded. 'Looks good. Everyone has a signature move these days: runners, Olympic cyclists, viral pop hits on the Internet. That can be ours.'

'Glad I'm behind the drums.' Tris smirked.

Anji tugged his sleeve. 'You know, Tris, I think you should do the heart thing too when we do – with your drumsticks crossed in a kiss. You can't look cool or we might win.'

The boy with a guitar who went before them played far beyond his allotted five minutes, performing a melancholy piece about his break-up with a girlfriend and the end of the world. He was received with muted applause from the audience.

Standing in the wings, still with his coat over his embarrassing costume, Leo listened in on the judges' comments.

'Well, I can see that was heartfelt,' said the first judge. Zane Jackson ran the *Star Makers* show and could make or break a career. He grinned a big toothy smile to camera and flicked back his dark brown hair. 'But I don't think the public are quite ready for you yet. I'm afraid that's a "No!" from me.'

The second judge, Sadie Hunter, a sharply-dressed

blonde singer with an impressive recording career behind her, sat back, fingers drumming on the arms of her big red armchair. 'I can see you have talent, Doug, but on this one I have to agree with Zane. We want someone with that star power and I'm afraid you just don't have the potential to fit that profile.'

The boy sloped off-stage, dragging his instrument. Leo thought it a fair result. Doug would do much better busking in subways and at local bars feeling persecuted by the music industry rather than trying to make it in the glittery world of *Star Makers*. It suited his style.

The assistant director rushed up. 'Ready, guys?'

Leo nodded and slipped off his coat. The woman did a double take when she saw the pink sweater. She checked her list.

'I've got your name right, have I? You are The Cutie Pies?'

'I'm afraid so,' said Tris sourly.

Leo asked himself for the millionth time just why he had dragged his friends into this. Oh yeah: tickets. He had sold his soul for a muddy campsite and amazing music. He suddenly felt a lot better.

The assistant's face brightened when she spotted Bones. 'Oh, you have a dog, do you? The public always like pets.'

Bones growled as she approached to stroke him. She gave a little laugh. 'Nervous are you, sweetie?'

'His name is Bones,' said Tris.

'Great, just great: The Cutie Pies and their dog, Bows. It has a ring to it.' Her walkie-talkie beeped. 'That's your cue. Good luck.'

Exchanging a wry look, the four stepped on to the stage into the pulsating lights.

'And here we have some of our youngest entrants on today's list!' burbled the presenter. Leo recognized a local TV personality, Jamie Custor, more often seen doing the weather report; the producers only ran to B-list celebrities for the opening rounds of the show. Leo looked again at Jamie. Make that C-list. 'Give a big warm welcome to The Cutie Pies and their faithful hound, Bows!'

Enthusiastic applause and a few titters of laughter lightened the leaden atmosphere that still lingered after the last act.

'And I believe they are going to sing a song they've composed themselves. What's it called?'

Leo found a microphone thrust under his nose. He was aware of his bandmates taking their places around him.

'It's called 'Fluffy Kitten'.' He looked down at his bright blue trousers with their decoration of rainbows and pink unicorns.

'Sounds ... um ... sweet.' Jamie retreated to the edge of the stage. 'Take it away, guys.'

Leo strummed the first few chords, Anji harmonizing with a little 'la-la-la' line Dan had added. His cue arrived.

'Oh Kitten, you are the sweetest,
Oh Kitten, you are the best,
I want to wrap you up in rainbows
And cuddle you to my chest.'

Anji made the heart shape. The drum beat paused.
She turned to glare at Tris until finally, reluctantly,
he did the same with crossed sticks. There was a
ripple of friendly laughter in the audience. Leo had
been hoping for boos.

And now came the chorus. Anji took the melody
as Leo sang the harmony:

'So fluffy, uffy, wuffy,
So fluffy, uffy, wuffy,
Kitten, we love you,
Oo-oo-oo-oo.'

Bones howled – probably in agony.

There was much more like that – too much. Leo was feeling depressed well before the last chord faded. Just in time he remembered they were all supposed to pose making heart shapes.

Silence.

Then rapturous applause and sobs from some of the older ladies in the audience. Shading his eyes, Leo realized that half the crowd was made up of pensioners bussed in for the afternoon, munching on digestive biscuits and sipping tea from vacuum flasks. Near the front, wiping tears from her eyes, was their mum, hands clasped to her chest. She was mouthing: 'My babies!'

Oh good grief!

Jamie bounced forward, taking his prompt from the reaction in the room.

'Wow, that was amazing! And they wrote it all themselves, ladies and gentlemen. Judges, what do you think?'

Zane sat back in his chair, his expression hard to read until he broke into a broad smile.

'That's the best act we've seen so far today – fresh, youthful, original. The whole cute element is so different from the hard edge most go for. A big *Star Makers* "Yes!" from me!'

Leo's hopes rested on Sadie. She looked perplexed. 'Most unexpected. Love the dog.'

Bones pricked up his ears.

'They certainly have something, so yeah, I'm going to agree with Zane on this one. It's a "Yes!" from me.'

'Are you sure?' squeaked Anji.

'Yes, yes I am. Well done. We look forward to seeing you in the semi-final.'

Jamie stepped forward, eager to move the show along. 'Another round of applause, please, for The Cutie Pies and their dog, Bows.' He gestured for them to make their exit. Still stunned, the four traipsed off-stage.

'How could that have gone so wrong?' asked Leo. 'We were just terrible.'

'We made a fatal error.' Tris whipped off his sweater and stuffed it in the bag. 'We forgot that the public has rotten taste. Pink sells well for a reason.'

'Bury me now. I will never be able to face school again.' Leo handed his jumper to Dan. 'Burn that.'

Anji took the bow off Bones' collar. 'I didn't see anyone I knew – apart from Mum. We were on quite late so I think most people had already played and gone.'

'One bright spot in a disaster,' muttered Dan. 'Let's sleep on it, then work out what we are going to do about this.'

Chapter 4

Crisis meeting

The next day was a sunny Sunday morning so the band took their meeting out to the park.

'What was the matter with our plan?' asked Leo, dragging his feet on the ground beneath the swing.

Tris tied Bones up outside the playground and left him with a stick to chew. 'We should've seen it coming.'

'But it's getting worse.' Leo kicked against the ground to give himself a push. 'Our mum was so pleased, she's bought the tickets to Glastonbury. She thinks we've agreed to stick with the competition all the way through and is already working on the costumes for the semi-final. She's unstoppable.'

Anji swung next to Leo. 'She'll hit the roof if we pull out.'

'No, it's worse than that: she'll be really, really sad.'

Dan leaned on one of the struts of the swing set. 'Same at my house. My parents are so proud. They're going to come to the next round.'

Tris grinned at his three friends, not sharing their

parental problems. 'Whereas my dad was horrified we got through. No son of a Dead Head should be in *Star Makers*, he claims. He says he's disowning me.'

'What?' Leo stopped swinging.

'It's a joke.' Tris frowned. 'I think.'

Dan slapped him on the back. 'There's always a spare floor in my bedroom if he kicks you out.'

'You're all heart, Dan.'

'So what do you want to do?' asked Leo. 'Let's take a band vote the usual way. Drums?'

Tris grimaced. 'You know what I think.'

'Bass?'

Dan looked at Anji, then the sky, and finally Leo. 'Once more – for Mum and Dad.'

'Guitar?'

Anji nodded.

As the frontman of the band, Leo decided it was his responsibility to cast the deciding vote.

'OK, my view is that we go ahead for a final time. We'll need to make sure we absolutely fail.'

Tris groaned but accepted the majority decision with a shrug. 'You're all mad, but all right.'

'It was bad luck there were so many grannies in the

crowd,' said Dan. 'If it had been a different audience, they would have booed us off-stage.'

'They would have been right to do that,' muttered Tris. 'I wanted to boo myself.'

'The semi-final is always in a big venue. I bet the audience will be completely different,' said Anji hopefully.

'It'll be harder to hide though,' said Tris. 'There will be loads of TV cameras there.'

'Double the disguise,' suggested Dan, 'so even our mothers won't recognize us.'

'Our mum will – she's dressing us how she'd like us to be,' sighed Anji.

'I think our basic idea is OK,' Leo added. 'All we need to do is pile so much frosting on the cupcake that even someone with the sweetest tooth will get sick of us. We made a mistake with kittens – too many cat-lovers out there.'

Dan pulled out the old list and crossed off KITTENS. 'Let's look at this again. What's more annoying than that? More sugary. Suggestions, please.'

'Granulated, caster, demerara, golden syrup, maple syrup,' chanted Tris. Having been overruled, he wasn't in a constructive mood yet.

'*Helpful* suggestions.'

'Bunny wabbits,' said Anji.

Dan wrote it down. 'You mean rabbits.'

'No, *wabbits* – cute baby talk.'

'Lambs,' said Leo.

'Princesses, puppies, ducklings, ickle babies and foals,' added Tris.

'Not foals,' said Anji. 'Foals can be cool.'

Dan winked at her. 'OK, not foals. Puppies are OK but it's lame to sing about them. Same goes for any baby animals.'

'Heap up the sickly stuff and we will be hounded off the stage.' Leo began to feel confident this would work.

'And the really good news – the competition is so far away that no one round here will ever know.' Anji grabbed the list from Dan and gave it a big kiss. 'This is our recipe for success.'

'Don't you mean failure?' asked Dan.

'Same thing.'

They held covert practice sessions. They had agreed to make one change and that was to leave out Bones.

However, when the *Star Makers* producers got in touch, they insisted on the original line-up, including the dog. It appeared that the feedback from the crowd had been that even those who hadn't liked the song had loved Bones howling along. The next round would be televised so they wanted the novelty appeal for the audience sitting at home.

'It means another costume, Bones,' Anji told him sadly. His big brown eyes looked at her so trustingly. 'I'm thinking one of those dog ruffs and a tiara like you get on novelty calendars: *Dogs doing funny stuff*.'

'*Dogs being embarrassed by their owners*, you mean,' grumbled Tris. 'Do we have to?'

'Apparently we signed something when we entered the audition to say we wouldn't swap the members of our band. That's considered cheating,' explained Leo.

'Am I missing something here, but isn't Bones a dog? How can he be a member of The Cutie Pies?'

'Our official name is *The Cutie Pies and their Faithful Hound, Bows*, according to this letter.' Leo waved it in the air.

Tris and Bones exchanged a long look. 'This will deserve at least a year's supply of treats,' Tris decided.

'If we win, we'll be able to afford more than that,' said Dan.

'Shut up, Dan – winning is not our aim here.'

'Still, you know, aren't you the least bit tempted by the TV appearances and the recording contract?' mused Dan. 'I am.'

'No. I'm only going before a camera in heavy disguise, then The Cutie Pies will be killed off and I'm going to dance on their grave.' Tris demonstrated a little tap-dance.

Bones yipped his agreement.

Chapter 5
The semi-final

Mum drove Leo and Anji to the semi-final in the city, fizzing with excitement all the way. 'You have me to thank for all this!' She switched lanes, merrily tooting the other half of the band travelling in Tris' dad's van with the drum kit. Tris' father sat glumly at the wheel, looking about as happy as if his favourite leather trousers had just been given to a charity shop by mistake.

'Yeah, I know, Mum,' said Leo.

'When you're famous, I'll be able to say: that's my little boy and girl up there. Not that it's about the fame, of course.'

'No, of course not,' said Anji ironically.

'I just want you to enjoy yourselves.'

'Yeah, right,' muttered Leo.

'And if you lose, I don't want you to be upset.'

'We won't be upset,' promised Anji.

'That's the spirit.' Mum hummed a line from 'Fluffy Kitten' and pulled into the multi-storey car park at the back of the theatre.

The facilities at the city theatre were much better than at the leisure centre. The Cutie Pies were given a dressing room and some thoughtful person had left out a water bowl for Bones. Like knights suiting up for war, they put on their costumes. Mum had excelled herself this time, making the boys skinny trousers in sparkly silver material. They had chosen their own T-shirts, each with a different soppy slogan. Leo's said 'I love my mum' and was surrounded by daisies. Dan's had 'Kittens are cute', decorated with a little tabby peering over the edge of a teacup. Tris had printed 'Daddy's boy' on his over a picture of his father, just to annoy him. When Anji took off her jacket they saw that hers said 'Foals are cool' and had a stylish pattern of a horse running across the middle.

'What?' she asked when the boys stared accusingly.

'Your T-shirt. It isn't cheesy like ours,' said Tris.

She shrugged. 'So? I might get to wear it again, whereas none of you are going to put on a pink T-shirt after today, are you?'

'True. It'll fit in the line-up.' Dan was always on Anji's side. 'She's never going to look as silly as us, whatever we do. It's a boy-girl thing.'

'But at least she could try,' grumbled Leo.

Anji stuck her tongue out at him. 'I'm wearing a pink satin ribbon in my hair – I call that trying very hard.'

'Hey, guys!' Zanc Jackson bounced into the room. 'Ready for the show?'

'As we'll ever be,' said Tris.

'No need to be nervous, even though there is a crowd of two thousand out there, and your act will be shown on national TV, and there are lots of press, and you are our youngest and least experienced act to perform tonight. I'm sure you'll be fine.' With a sweep of his eyes, he checked their costumes. 'You really live up to your name.' His smile grew even broader when he saw Bones' tiara. 'Fabulous. Everyone will be rooting for you, you'll see.' He rushed out of the room.

'I rather wish they wouldn't,' said Leo to the door Zane closed behind him. 'I'd prefer them hooting with derision.'

Zane poked his head back round the door. 'Oh, I forgot to mention: we invited some supporters from your school to give you encouragement. Funny thing was they didn't seem to know anything about it. That's just so sweet of you all to be so shy!' He beamed at them. 'Anyway, as a special treat, we gave them free tickets and a bus to come here. They'll be in the front. Break a leg.' He darted back out into the corridor.

A deathly silence fell. Leo couldn't find the words to express his horror.

'Help,' said Anji.

Tris gave a croak deep in his throat. 'That is the sound of my reputation dying a horrible death.'

'Whose bright idea was this anyway?' asked Dan plaintively. 'Oh yeah, ours.'

Anji sat beside him and bumped shoulders. 'Look, we just go out, sing and then we deal with the fallout.'

'Yeah, easy.' Dan nudged her back.

There was no time to panic, tempting though that sounded. Leo stood up and rubbed his hands together. 'Look, guys, it'll only last five minutes and then, whatever happens, The Cutie Pies are history. Tris, are you still with us?'

Drawing on his last dregs of loyalty to the band, Tris clicked his fingers to Bones. 'Come on, my faithful hound. The scaffold awaits.'

The act before them was really good: a female singer-songwriter with a formidable voice and excellent piano playing. Dan tapped Leo on the back in relief. This was more like it. No one would choose them after hearing her.

When the applause died down, the judges gave their verdict, Sadie Hunter speaking first.

'Michaela, you really made that song your own. I think you've got something special, so that's a "Yes!" from me.'

Zane was frowning. Why on earth was he frowning? A truly talented performer had just entertained the room: he should be over the moon. 'Yeah, I agree that you show musical skill, but I don't know, haven't we all seen it before? There's nothing new here, nothing to stand out. I don't think we can get the listening public to take notice. No, that's going to take something really unique and fresh. Sorry, Michaela, but it's a "No!" from me.'

The audience gasped in astonishment. The presenter came forward, also shocked by the decision.

'Let me remind you that the verdict still puts Michaela in top position as she has both strong public support from the previous round and one of the judges on her side. So let's give Michaela a big *Star Makers* round of applause.'

The pianist walked gracefully off the far side of the stage. Leo wanted to copy Bones and howl in frustration. Zane had just blown away their best chance of failing.

And so the nightmare began ...

'And now we come to our last act of the evening. They are the youngest performers to get this far on any series of *Star Makers*, so make them feel welcome! They're a bit shy and didn't even tell their own friends that they were coming on the show!'

'Aw!' went the audience, not entirely without mockery from some.

The cameras zoomed in on the row of school children.

'Please let a meteor strike right now,' groaned Leo.

'I give you, The Cutie Pies and their Faithful Hound, Bows!'

Leo had a split second to register the stunned look on the faces of his classmates before he ran on-stage and that was the moment he realized that the domino had fallen. The calamity was inevitable.

'And they are going to perform a little song they have written themselves called 'Lost Bunny'.'

Leo closed his eyes but no missile from space put him out of his misery. Instead he started to play and bent closer to the microphone. What could he do but carry on with the plan?

'*I don't know where my bunny wabbit is today,*' he sang,

'*He's lost – he's gone far, far away.*
So if you find him, please send him back to me,
Bow round his neck like a present under the Christmas tree.'

There was much more of this deplorable stuff. He didn't dare look straight at them but he could just see the dumbfounded looks of  his classmates. They were embarrassed for the band and for the school. Some were hiding their heads behind their programmes or putting on their coats to disguise their uniform.

When the last awful verse wound up with the triumphant finding of the lost rabbit, the band waited for the verdict. The applause was warm, but not rapturous as it had been on their first performance.

Leo began to hope they had sickened everyone sufficiently for their band to be rejected. That wouldn't solve the issue of social death at school, but Leo could only cope with one disaster at a time.

'Thanks, guys. And now it's over to the judges,' said the presenter.

Sadie gave them a sympathetic smile. 'That was very sweet.'

'Sweet? We were the musical equivalent of tooth rot,' muttered Leo.

'You are clearly very talented and in a few years might well win this competition, but just at the moment I'd say you need a bit of seasoning. So, sadly, it's a "No!" from me. Sorry, Bows.'

Phew! The band tried not to look too pleased.

'Oh. What a shame,' said Anji, unable to muster a devastated look for the TV cameras.

Zane turned on his fellow judge. 'Oh, come on, Sadie, I disagree. They were epic! If you are looking for an act with star power, this is it! I can make money, I mean I can make good music with these youngsters. The older population is edged out of pop music. This band, appealing to the grandparents and parents, is just what we need at the present time. It is a huge *Star Makers* "Yes!" from me.'

No, it can't be! Bones howled. The band didn't know where to look: the front row was a no-go area, Zane was clearly insane, and Sadie incredulous.

The presenter jogged forward. 'And that leaves us with a cliffhanger, ladies and gentlemen – the judges are split between tonight's two most popular acts. Is it going to be Michaela, our talented singer-songwriter, or the uniquely sweet sound of The Cuties Pies?'

The pianist was ushered on to stand next to the band. Tris appeared as if he was about to burst, Incredible Hulk-like, out of his shiny, cute outfit at the injustice of being liked for being awful.

Dan had put his arm round Anji so she could bury her face in his chest. The crowd would interpret it as nerves; the band knew it was to muffle her screams.

'Sorry,' Leo muttered to Michaela. He'd really liked her act.

'So, judges, which is it going to be?' The presenter dropped his voice. 'And I'll remind the folks at home that your votes count as much as the judges'.'

There was a slow beat of the drums. 'The votes are in and have been counted and verified. Judges, your verdict first, please.'

Sadie smiled kindly at The Cutie Pies. 'I'm sorry, I still think Michaela deserves the chance. Cutie Pies, you are just too cute for me.'

Sensible woman, thought Leo. Why couldn't the rest of Great Britain be like her?

The presenter patted Michaela on the shoulder. 'Zane?'

The Star Maker spread his arms wide. 'You know what? I'm still backing the band. The Cutie Pies.'

The presenter handed over the results of the public vote. 'Then it's down to the public to decide.'

Zane flipped open the envelope and grinned. 'And the public is always right: it's gonna be ... The Cutie Pies!'

The crowd erupted in hysterical applause – all except the front row of classmates.

The presenter spoke to camera. 'So the nation has decided. The Cutie Pies go forward to the final. Good luck, Michaela. Despite losing out today, I'm sure we'll hear much more from you.'

The camera swooped in on the silent school kids and Leo could hear the commentary coming from the wings.

'*And the children from their school are sitting stunned in their seats. The Cutie Pies look as if they can't believe their ears*!'

Leo disagreed. His mates – make that *ex*-mates – did not look stunned; they looked like they wanted to gag the band.

Then the audience behind the front row moved to chanting: '*Make the sign*! *Make the sign*!'

The presenter nodded to them. 'Hey, kids, they want you to do the heart. Nice big smile as you pose for the cameramen.'

With all the enthusiasm of patients opening wide for the dentist's drill, The Cutie Pies made the heart sign on their chests. Cameras flashed.

'I think we can say we have a hit on our hands,' the presenter concluded as the theme music signalled the end of the programme.

Chapter 6
I Rock

Every newspaper in the land carried a front page picture of the band posing with their heart sign. The write-up inside varied from a gushing 'We love these fresh-faced youngsters!' to the bitter 'Has *Star Makers* finally gone too far with these sugar-coated lyrics?' Mum, of course, had bought a copy of every one and was busy making a scrapbook, blithely unaware of the trauma her children were going through.

'That was the TV station calling,' she told them as Anji and Leo sat before the pile of papers. 'They want to do an interview.'

'Fine,' said Leo dully.

'They'll pick you up tomorrow and you can make your appearance on the evening show.'

'OK,' said Anji.

Neither had even a tingle of excitement about appearing on television.

'I'll have to work out what you should wear.' Mum shook out the costumes she had washed. 'These won't do. They've seen these already.'

'Jeans – we should wear ordinary stuff,' said Leo quickly.

'Yes, that's probably best.' Mum draped the silver trousers over the clothes horse. 'It's a good idea to show the audience that under the costumes you are just normal children.'

'No, under the costumes we are doomed kids because we are not going to survive school today,' muttered Leo.

Anji poured him a bowl of cereal and nudged it in front of him. He raised a brow in surprise.

'You're not eating,' she said.

His little sister worrying about him: that was new. 'Who are you and what have you done with Anji?'

She gave him a weak smile. 'Do you think it was my T-shirt that did it? I mean, all I ever wanted was to be in an edgy band with a cult following and now I'm worried I've made us a mainstream success.'

He hadn't realized his sister had been blaming herself. 'No, Anji, it wasn't your fault. I think Zane had decided we were going to win before we went on-stage. He's not concerned about the fact our music is rubbish; he just thinks he can sell us.'

'Yes, I got that when he swallowed 'Lost Bunny' without flinching.'

They crunched mouthfuls of cereal in companionable misery.

'What are we going to do?' she asked.

'I guess we have two problems. The first is school.' Anji shuddered. 'The second is what to do about the final. Let's take them one by one.'

Anji's phone pinged. 'I've got a text from Dan. He wants to meet us before we go in today.'

'He probably thinks there's safety in numbers.'

'Maybe, but he says he's had an idea.'

'His last idea was to wear his granny's jumpers and look how well that turned out.'

Anji shrugged. 'We can't talk. We were the ones who set the ball rolling.'

'OK, let's go and hear what he has to say.'

They met up under the railway bridge, sunglasses on, hoods up. The wall was slimy and black with dirt, graffiti zigzagged across the bricks, a dank puddle gathered at their feet – heaven after the sugar-pink success of The Cutie Pies.

'I couldn't sleep last night,' Dan began.

'Neither could I,' said Tris. 'Dad was really angry.'

'Not with you, surely?' asked Leo.

'No, with the whole nation who voted for us. He said they had no more brains than a jellyfish.'

'Jellyfish don't have brains.'

'Exactly.'

'As I was saying,' said Dan, 'I couldn't sleep. I was thinking that we might even win this competition if things go on this way.' He didn't look as upset at the prospect as Leo expected. 'And it struck me at about two in the morning that the answer is obvious.'

'It is?' Anji frowned. 'Not seeing it, Dan.'

'I rock.' He folded his arms as if expecting them to applaud.

'Don't kid yourself,' muttered Tris.

'Not me, Tris! It's a style of music I've just invented.'

Anji wrinkled her nose. 'I don't get it. What do you mean?'

Leo was glad Anji had asked the question because it was exactly what he was thinking.

'I Rock stands for "ironic rock". You know what irony is, right?'

'I think so. It's where you say one thing but mean

another, like "Wow, that's a really lovely unicorn duvet cover – just what I needed."'

Dan frowned. 'I told you that you can change your Christmas present at the shop. I won't be offended.'

'Already have.'

'Yeah, her bed is now covered in vampires,' said Leo. 'Mum's not pleased.'

'Can we get back to social death, guys?' Tris checked the time. 'We've only got five minutes to come up with a plan before the bell rings.'

'That *is* the plan. Ironic rock.' Dan shook his head at their blank faces. 'I can't believe you don't get it.'

'Explain to us in simple words,' said Leo.

'All right. We don't like The Cutie Pies and only did it to please our parents, correct?'

'Yes, we were bribed into doing it,' agreed Leo.

'So it was all an act?'

'Yep.'

'But everyone thinks we did it seriously, that our musical taste has suddenly gone as sweet and sickly as marshmallows.'

'You're not telling us anything we don't already know,' said Tris.

'So the answer is we say we have started a new kind of fashion for ironic rock, or I Rock: be something you absolutely hate and see if anyone gets the joke.'

Leo pondered that for a moment. 'So we can say that they are the idiots if they didn't see through it? I like it.'

'Makes us even cooler than we were before, because only a select number would get the joke,' Dan explained.

'Select number being everyone in our school, as they won't want to be uncool,' said Anji.

'That's right.'

'I get it,' said Tris. 'I suppose it's either that or we run away to Australia.'

'I think they've got *Star Makers* in Australia too,' Anji said despondently.

'Then somewhere without television – Antarctica maybe.'

'Guys,' interrupted Dan, 'the point I'm trying to make is that we embrace The Cutie Pies and make this work for us.'

'Dan, it's brilliant.' Anji took off her sunglasses and pushed back her hood. 'I think I can persuade my year to convert to I Rock. They all like to be first in any new craze.'

'Great. How about you two?'

Leo and Tris looked at each other then nodded.

'It's a plan,' said Tris. 'We'll only know if it's worked if we survive the day.'

The bell rang, the sound carrying to their spot just out of sight of the school gates.

'Let's do it.' Dan held out his fist. The other three all bumped it with their knuckles. 'I Rock, yeah?'

'I Rock,' they agreed.

'We report back after school?' said Leo. He was hoping Dan was an undiscovered genius, but feared this brainwave might end up as flat as a hedgehog on a motorway, run over by the mockery of their classmates.

Tris nodded. 'I think we'll know earlier than that, but yeah, let's meet here after last lesson.'

Anji had to confront her year alone, but she didn't seem too concerned as she hurried off to her classroom for registration.

'See you later!' she called, bounding up to her friends. They gave her a cool reception, but she was soon defrosting their attitude.

Leo, Tris and Dan slouched into their form room. The excited buzz died as soon as they came in.

'Hi, guys,' said Leo, as if he was oblivious to what everyone was thinking.

'Hey, it's The Cutie Pies!' crowed Richard, one of Leo's least favourite people in the form. 'Hey, losers, gonna sing to us about bunny wabbits?'

Leo shrugged. 'If you like. I thought we really killed it on Saturday.' He sat down and kicked back from the desk. 'I mean, I'm amazed we got through it without laughing.'

Charlie, Richard's best friend, wrinkled his forehead in confusion. 'Laughing? What do you mean?'

Leo sat forward with a thump. 'Don't tell me you took it seriously?' He turned to Dan. 'Can you believe it? They fell for it like everyone else!'

Dan snorted and took out his phone, dismissing Richard and Charlie.

Tris nudged Carmen who sat next to him. 'I bet you didn't make that mistake, hey?'

She opened her mouth, then decided just to shake her head.

'See, Carmen got the joke.'

'What joke?' growled Richard.

'Yep, they fell for it.' Leo winked at Carmen. 'It's new thing – I Rock.'

'Ironic rock,' said Dan and Tris together.

'Never heard of it,' said Charlie.

Tris leaned towards Charlie. 'You send up everything you hate. You become like an anti-rock star, so bad that only really dim people believe in it.'

'But the public voted for you,' said Carmen.

'Yeah, it's a win-win approach – a few were in on the joke and voted ironically; the others like The Cutie Pies and that just tells you everything you need to know about people who watch *Star Makers*. You got that, didn't you, Carmen?'

Their classmate did not want to look slow. 'Oh, sure I did. I told everyone it was clearly one huge joke. Didn't I?'

'Nope, I really don't remember that,' said Richard, shaking his head. 'I remember you saying you'd never be seen in public with any of The Cutie Pies again.'

'But I was just being ironic!' she said triumphantly.

'So was I,' Charlie added swiftly.

That just left Richard unconvinced. 'How long is this I Rock joke of yours going to last?'

'We'll have to see. I Rock reinvents itself the whole time.' Dan laced his hands behind his head and whistled a bar of 'Lost Bunny'.

Tris scowled at him. 'It was for one performance only. The Cutie Pies joke is dead and buried.'

Uh-oh. Leo assessed the situation and realized they had a problem. Tris may have backed I Rock to save their reputation, but he had no intention of going any further, not even with the sparkling promise of fame and fortune at the end of the road.

Chapter 7
When friends fall out ...

i was waiting for the boys after school. 'That was ᵗreat! My whole year bought into the idea of I Rock.' Even in her good mood, the silence between Dan and Tris warned her all was not well. 'Problem? Did they not believe you in your year?'

Leo hooked Anji's arm to pull her away from their friends so he could explain. 'Everyone believed it.'

'So what's the matter?' She glanced over her shoulder at Dan and Tris who were following on behind.

'The future of The Cutie Pies. Let's get Tris and Dan back to ours and see if we can divert the bust-up they are about to have.'

'Bust-up? What bust-up?' Anji sighed. 'And I was having such a good day.'

Leo raided the emergency biscuit tin and put it in the centre of the table between the warring parties. Maybe chocolate would put them in a better mood?

'Drink?' asked Anji brightly, pretending Tris and Dan didn't look as though they were about to go for each other. Tris had his angry birds face on but Dan was barricaded in his fort with his helmet intact. Anji put a carton of juice on the table and shoved glasses within reach of both boys. 'How was your day, Leo?'

'Mine was fine. Played football in PE.'

'That's good.'

The brother and sister exchanged looks. They did not normally talk like this. Airy chit-chat was not part of the evening routine; fighting for the TV remote was more the order of the day.

'So, what's the matter?' Anji prompted.

'Grrr,' said Tris.

'He's so stubborn!' Dan crushed a biscuit into pieces. 'He can't see that we've got an amazing opportunity. All we have to do is carry on for another week and we might end up with a recording contract.'

Anji frowned. 'Oh. I thought we'd stumble on and do the final but I guess Tris isn't happy with that?'

'Not happy?' Tris shot off his seat like a firework. 'I'm furious – mad – livid – and every other word for enraged that you can find in the dictionary.'

He jabbed a finger at Leo. 'You promised me that we'd kill off The Cutie Pies. I was planning to dance on their grave – or at least on that stupid T-shirt – but Mr Blinded-by-fame here is seriously considering carrying on!'

'So? We'd be fools not to give it a go,' Dan shot back.

'That wasn't the deal.'

'But we didn't even consider what would happen if we won, did we?' said Anji.

Dan rapped the table. 'Wrong: I did. I said it was tempting, didn't I? No other kids our age get offered the chance to make an album. Anji, I know you've never gone for popularity, but can't you see we'd be working with professionals and we'd learn so much?'

'I suppose so.' Anji grinned. 'I might have to rethink that cult following thing though.'

'But you're missing the point, Dan. It's not us they'll make an album with – it's The Cutie Pies,' Tris fumed. 'Yes, I want to be a musician, but not like this. We'd never be taken seriously again.'

'But we'll create a fan base, become well known.' Dan had an eager gleam in his eye, in sharp contrast to glowering Tris. 'We can shift our style once we make our name. We could even see if I Rock catches on – make the strategy public.'

Leo rubbed his neck wearily. 'I'm not sure I can see the shift between 'Lost Bunny' and our real sound – it's a bit of a stretch – and I think I Rock will just annoy most people.'

'None of that matters because I'm not putting myself through that again,' Tris stated. 'Not even for you, Dan. And I'm speaking as the fifth member of the band's owner. Bones is going to regain his dignity – no more Bows or dumb costumes.'

'But we signed an agreement with the television people!' protested Dan.

'That reminds me, we have an appearance tomorrow night,' muttered Leo.

'No, we don't.' Tris shook his head. 'And what are they going to do if we don't show up in any case? Sue us? We're kids. Nothing we've signed can possibly be binding.'

'But this is our chance, Tris. You're being selfish, not thinking of us.' Dan swept his hand round in a gesture including Leo and Anji.

'Enough with the emotional blackmail, Dan. The Cutie Pies are finished.' Tris stood up. 'You have to choose between fame or your friend. I'm not going to change my mind.' He walked out.

In the awkward silence that followed, Anji put the lid back on the biscuit tin. 'That went well.'

'I see you've got this irony thing mastered.' Dan sipped his drink, trying to disguise his upset. 'Does anyone know any other drummers?'

'Tris does have a point,' said Leo. 'We did promise. And if we keep on doing this act then one day we'll find we are not just pretending to be The Cutie Pies, but we *are* The Cutie Pies.'

'So you're siding with him, are you?' Dan took this suggestion further than Leo meant.

'What? No! I'm just saying that he makes sense.'

'And I don't? Anji, do you think I'm wrong?'

This put Anji in a very awkward spot. 'We do keep saying that this is the last time, then something else happens. It's a bit risky to carry on.'

'Not you too? I thought I could count on you to understand, but you choose them over me.'

Anji was really upset at the accusation she was

being disloyal to Dan in some way, especially since they had been on the verge of going out. She looked close to tears, but was just managing to hold on.

'Dan, you can't talk to Anji like that!' said Leo.

But Dan was too upset to feel sorry. 'Fine, I'm going. I know where I stand when brother and sister start ganging up on me.' He stormed out, slamming the door behind him

Leo put his arm around Anji's shoulder. 'Sorry my friends are being such idiots.'

'Your friends are always idiots.'

'Worse idiots than normal, I mean.'

'Thanks, Leo.' Anji gave a shuddering sigh. 'So, what are we going to tell Mum?'

'Nothing just yet. Let's see what they're like tomorrow at school. You and I can do the TV spot without them if they're still at war.'

'What are we going to say to the TV interviewer about the future of the band?'

'That this has all come as a big surprise and we don't know what's going to happen. It's the truth.'

'OK. Do you think Tris will let Bones come?'

'Probably, as long as he doesn't have to dress up.'

'Tris or Bones?'

'Both.'

Chapter 8
Dog fight

Tris and Dan were still not speaking to each other the next day. Leo felt like he was the umpire in a grudge match, being appealed to for his verdict on the idiotic behaviour of the other player.

'You know what I realized last night, Leo? Dan has dire taste in music. How can he even think that any of us would want to do that sickly stuff again? 'Fluffy Kitten', 'Lost Bunny' – major ugh factor!' That was Tris at break time as he scowled across the playground at Dan.

'Hmm,' said Leo.

'Tris is so full of himself!' raged Dan as he threw a few hoops at lunchtime in the basketball court. 'He can't just treat it all as a joke and take what's being offered. Instead he has to guard his precious reputation!' He lobbed the ball but it bounced off the ring and into Leo's hands. 'I mean, friends go out on a limb for friends, don't they? But does he? No.'

'Hmm,' said Leo, bouncing the ball twice and putting it through the hoop.

Tris took the last chair by Leo in maths, leaving Dan to find his own spot on the far side of the classroom. 'Look at him! I can't believe we let him in our band. Sure, he can compose a decent tune, but he's so out for himself, it's not true!'

'Uh-huh,' said Leo.

He waited a beat for Tris to unpack his textbooks. 'Is it OK if Anji and I take Bones with us to the TV interview?'

'Yeah, as long as I don't have to go and you don't say we're going to carry on with the competition.'

'It's just a chat with the brother and sister in the band, nothing big.'

'OK. Fetch him after school then.'

At the end of school, Dan cornered Leo. 'Are you still doing that TV thing?'

'Yes – just Anji and me. The producers said they understood that we had ... um ... creative tensions to sort out and couldn't all appear.'

Dan grabbed his sleeve. 'Promise you won't say we're pulling out of the performance on Saturday.'

'But we can't do it – not without Tris.'

Dan hunched his shoulders. 'Who needs him?

He is so full of himself, thinking his drumming is so important. I can't believe we let him into the band.'

'Hmm. Funny you should say that.'

'What?'

'Um, nothing.'

'Promise?'

'OK. We won't say anything at all either way.'

'Good enough.'

The limo picked up Anji and Leo then stopped at Tris' house so they could collect Bones. He was wearing his normal studded collar and was very pleased to see them if his madly wagging tail was anything to go by.

'Someone likes all the attention,' said Anji.

'Yeah, unlike his owner,' said Leo. The car pulled away and they waved to Tris who made a mocking heart sign to wish them luck. 'Odd: when he does that it seems more like a threat than a love sign, like he's promising that we will have our hearts ripped out of our chests if we revive The Cutie Pies.'

'And that is why he is your friend. You like his dark side.' Anji pulled Bones on to her lap. 'How are we going to help Dan and Tris make up? I mean, under it all, they're good friends. It's just that Dan is ready to take a short cut for a recording contract and Tris wants to do it the hard way.'

'Anji, you sound tempted yourself.'

'Well, I am. Dan's I Rock strategy was just so cool – edgy while letting us play in the mainstream. What about you?'

'I don't know what I think anymore. Yeah, winning is really tempting now it's a real possibility, but I hate the fact Dan and Tris are fighting.' Leo felt exhausted by all the complications.

'And we are a good band. We played those awful songs really well. We wouldn't have won if we didn't have some basic level of talent.'

'But the bad news is the band will be history if we don't get this sorted.'

Leo and Anji waited backstage for their cue to enter the studio.

'Bones, you'll behave, won't you?' Anji asked.

The dog sat heavily on his rump and a deep growl rumbled in his chest. His nose was pointing towards the stage, skin quivering with excitement.

Anji turned to Leo. 'Is that a yes or a no?'

'No idea.'

'Something has caught his attention.' Bones stood up and pulled on his leash. 'Easy, boy.'

Leo knelt down and took the dog's muzzle in his hand to get his attention. 'Power down those rockets, Bones. This is not the right time for you to go stratospheric on us.'

A green light flashed in front of them, giving them their cue.

'And now I am delighted to welcome the latest pop sensation. Please give a big hand for Leo and Anji of The Cutie Pies.'

Leo winced at the all too familiar name. The studio audience applauded as they entered, Anji trying to slow Bones down as he pulled her towards the centre of the stage. They reached the red sofa but Bones didn't want to stop. There was something on the far side that had his hackles rising.

'Hi, Anji, Leo,' said Simon Lemar, a sandy-haired man with a smug grin. 'And this is Bows?'

Neither confirming nor denying anything, even names, was the only way Leo could keep both his friends.

Actually, he's Tris' dog.'

'Tris being the drummer?'

'That's right.' Leo could see that Anji was having difficulty making Bones sit. The camera came for a close-up on him to give her a moment.

'So where are the other two members of The Cutie Pies tonight?'

'Homework crisis,' said Leo, grabbing for the first excuse he could think up.

'Aw, isn't that cute! You put homework over fame and fortune. No wonder so many voted for you – you really are the perfect kids. Let's have a look at you in action last weekend.' Simon signalled for the clip to run. The nice public Simon transformed into his true snide self once the cameras were turned away. 'What's the matter with that dog?' he muttered tetchily as the recording of 'Lost Bunny' began.

'I'm sorry,' whispered Anji, 'but he can smell something. Who was on last?'

'The winner of the National Dog Obedience Trials. Don't tell me they haven't cleared the studio?' He flapped his hands like a chicken flustered by a fox. 'I warned my ignoramus of a producer not to put two dogs on the same show, but would he listen?' Simon suddenly switched to a sunny smile as the footage ended. 'Here we are folks, talking to Leo and Anji, the favourites to win *Star Makers*.'

'Favourites!' exclaimed Anji.

'Joking?' asked Leo.

'Didn't you know? You're the favourites to win, thanks to the solid support from Zane Jackson. Tell me, what do you think Zane sees in you?'

Money, thought Leo sourly. 'I guess we're different from other acts he has backed in the past.'

'And how did you come up with the idea for The Cutie Pies? It's very brave of you to risk teasing. Not every boy would want to be seen in public in pink.'

How could he answer? wondered Leo. It would have to be another half truth. 'We wanted to stand out from the crowd.'

'You sure do. So, are you looking forward to the final?'

'It's going to be ... ' Leo struggled to reconcile his promise to his two mates.

'It's a step into the unknown,' said Anji swiftly. *Thank you, little sister.*

'I really don't know how it will turn out.' Anji tugged Bones away from sniffing the table leg with intent.

'What are you planning to sing?'

'Oh.' Leo looked at Anji.

'Leo's full of ideas, aren't you, bruv?' she said happily – and let go of the lead. Taking off like a

rocket, Bones shot to the far side of the studio.
'Oops, my bad.'

There was a growling, a howling and a scuffle in
the wings. Flushed out of hiding, two soundmen ran
across the back of the set holding long microphones
like pole vaulters taking a jump.

'Looks like we have some technical difficulties,
folks,' Simon said with a static grin.

'I think Bones has found a friend,' said Leo dryly.

The winner of the National Dog Obedience
Trials bounded across the stage, pursued by Bones.
His owner followed, screaming for her dog to
'Behave!' The collie jumped over the sofa and
knocked the drinking glasses off the low table,
showering Simon's lap with water. Bones followed,

landing with a sliding thump on the wet table, surfing stylishly off the end to continue his pursuit.

'Perhaps we had better go and help,' suggested Anji.

Simon nodded frantically as a camera went swinging in a circle to capture the dogfight. 'Yes, sorry to end it here folks, but you can see The Cutie Pies on Saturday.'

'Or maybe not,' muttered Leo.

'So, goodnight.' The camera light switched off and the end credits rolled.

Simon collapsed back in his chair. 'You poisonous little girl – you did that on purpose! I thought you were meant to be sweet!'

'Appearances can be deceptive,' Anji smiled angelically.

Chapter 9
What are friends for?

Anji and Leo returned home late that night in the back of the limo, Bones sleeping at their feet having seen off the dog competition. Brother and sister were extremely happy with each other. Facing trouble brought them together; shame that wasn't the case with their two friends.

'What are we going to do about Tris and Dan?' Anji asked.

'Don't know,' admitted Leo.

'And Saturday – what do we do about the final?'

'Same answer squared.'

'I just wish we could turn time back and start this over again. We've made so many mistakes.'

'They call that twenty-twenty hindsight.'

'Wouldn't it be cool if we could all be friends *and* mega famous.' She settled against his shoulder to take a nap. 'I really miss Dan.'

Leo hated to see Anji's relationship with Dan get caught in the crossfire. He rubbed Bones' tummy with his toe. The dog turned over, bent legs stuck in the air. He let out a funny little whimper of contentment. *Maybe, just maybe*, thought Leo, he did have a solution. Risky though. If it went wrong, he might lose both of his friends.

Leo cornered Tris at school on Friday lunchtime. 'OK, I've had enough of you and Dan being mad at each other.'

Tris dumped his leftovers in the recycling bin. 'He started it.'

'I'm not sure who started it but I'm going to end it. Come with me.' He grabbed Tris and towed him to the bike sheds. The kids who approached to wish them luck in the competition soon sensed the stormy atmosphere around the two boys, backtracked and left them alone. 'I'll come right out with it: what makes a friend?'

'Everything Dan isn't.' Tris folded his arms defensively. 'A friend is loyal, respects your opinions, keeps their word.'

'Agreed. So, first question: are you Dan's friend?'

'Was.'

'Take a good look in the mirror, Tris. Did you listen to Dan?'

'But he gave me his word ... '

'No, *I* said that we were going to end The Cutie Pies. I don't think he ever said anything about it at all.'

'But he knew what I thought!'

'And you knew he was thinking about winning.'

Tris frowned.

'Remember how all this started? Dan went out on a limb for me and Anji. He was prepared to go to Loserville because we asked him to do it. He showed he was our friend.'

'So did I.'

'Yeah, but only when he threatened to carry you in kicking and screaming. All he wants is to see if we can all get something from the win. He's not thinking just about himself, but all of us.'

'No, he's mainly thinking about Anji,' said Tris grumpily.

Leo grimaced. 'Yeah, OK, maybe he's gone a bit crazy, what with liking my sister and everything, but that's not my point. How much would it hurt you, really, if we did this one more time? Bones wouldn't mind. Anji and I are happy to give it a go. It's just down to you now.'

Leo walked away quickly before Tris had time to argue back.

The next target, Dan, was spotted at the end of school. Leo jogged to catch up with him.

'Avoiding me?'

'Yeah, well, you and Tris were ganging up on me so I thought I'd steer clear.'

'By "ganging up" do you mean not immediately agreeing with you?'

'I suppose I do.'

'That's a bit ironic, isn't it? Because you could say that you are ganging up on us by not taking our view.'

'I don't think you can be a gang of one.'

'You're making a very good attempt at it. Anji is really upset that you're not speaking to her. I'm not exactly over the moon this week to find myself frozen out. Even Tris is looking miserable.'

'It's his fault.'

'How exactly? He is only doing what he said he was going to do – pull out after the semi-final. Why are you surprised that he's sticking to his word?'

'But he's passing up this amazing chance. We can't go there tomorrow and just tell them we aren't singing in the final and that The Cutie Pies have disbanded.'

'Why can't we? Is the slim chance at fame and fortune worth losing Tris?' Leo judged it time to move on quickly, so Dan could think about that. 'Oh look, there's Anji. I'll just go catch up with her. See you later.'

'Yeah, later.'

When Leo looked back he was very pleased to see Dan trudging along with his hands dug deep in his pockets, lost in thought.

'What's the news on them?' asked Anji. She tossed her head when she caught Dan gazing after her longingly, too proud to let him see she cared.

'Have to see. Tomorrow we'll have an answer.'

'Are we still showing up at the final?'

'Yes.'

'To sing?'

'No idea. Look, do you feel like writing a different set of words to 'Lost Bunny'?'

'Why?'

'Just in case.'

Chapter 10

Final Chance

Anji and Leo lurked nervously in their dressing room as the last preparations were going on for the *Star Makers* final. Thanks to the television pictures of the auditorium they could see the crowd gathering. Their mum had a special seat near the front with the other finalists' families and just in case people didn't know who she was, she was wearing a T-shirt with their faces on it and the slogan 'I'm their mum'. If they hadn't already embarrassed themselves much more than that with their costumes in the earlier rounds, they would have refused to face the public ever again. The band's classmates had also started arriving. Leo had spotted that all of them were wearing I Rock badges.

'Do you think either of them will show up?' asked Anji.

'Don't know. I did my best but I said it would be a long shot.'

'And if they don't?'

'I'll go out and apologize to everyone. You don't need to do that. Stay here.'

'Uh-uh.' Anji shook her head. 'We're in this together, big brother. I'll go with you. We face the music together.'

'Thanks, Anji.'

There was a knock at the door and one of the assistants put his head into the room.

'Thirty minutes to go, guys – you'd better start getting changed. Where are the rest of you?'

'Running late,' said Leo; fingers crossed that that was the real explanation and not that they weren't coming at all.

'You realize this is live, don't you? I'll have to let the management know. Maybe we can shuffle you down the order.'

'Thanks. We'd appreciate it.' Anji gave him one of her sweetest and most irresistible smiles.

'OK, I'll get right on it. Good luck. My mum's a big fan.' He closed the door.

Leo and Anji exchanged a glance. There was nothing they could do to stop the approaching catastrophe. It was up to Tris and Dan now.

Slow footsteps stopped outside the door and it cracked open. Dan's head appeared cautiously in the gap.

'Dan!' Anji squawked, then tried to look cool as if she hadn't just given herself away.

'Oh good, you're here.' Dan slipped inside and made straight for Anji. 'I wasn't sure if you were going to show up.'

'We can't just not show up,' said Leo. 'We owe it to these people as they did give us the chance.'

'That's what I felt. I'm sorry, Anji. Forgive me?'

'Dan, you've been an idiot.' She walked into his arms.

'Thanks.' He gave her a hug that lifted her off her feet. Leo guessed the status of 'almost going out' had just become 'officially dating'. Leo now noticed that Dan wasn't in costume. His strategy had worked on Dan at least. 'So you've decided that The Cutie Pies are dead then?'

Dan put Anji down but kept his arm around her shoulders. 'Yes. We can't do it without Tris – that wouldn't be right. I've just come to say sorry to everyone who supported us. It's going to be ugly.'

With a scratch at the door, Bones padded inside.

'Talk about ugly!' said Leo.

'What are you wearing, you poor dog!' cried Anji.

Bones had a fluffy turquoise feather crown on his head and a tutu around his tubby middle.

'That's nothing compared to his owner,' said Tris glumly. He walked in wearing a glitter suit of pink – pink shirt, pink jacket, pink trousers, pink socks, pink shoes. 'I thought if we were going to do this one more time then I might as well totally kill off my street cred. Quick death rather than a lingering one.' He now realized none of the others were in costume. He frowned. 'Why aren't you ready?'

Dan's mouth was hanging open. Anji gave him a nudge.

'Say something,' she hissed.

'You did this for me?' Dan asked.

Tris looked awkward. 'Yeah. For all of us, really. Who cares if people laugh at us?'

'You care.'

'I did, but then I decided I'd got my priorities mixed up. We're a band. We do this together or not at all. So, same question: why aren't you ready?'

Leo grinned. 'Because we had decided to do what you want – kill off The Cutie Pies tonight and apologize for dropping out.'

Even Dan?'

'Yes.'

'I couldn't do it without you, mate.' Dan shook his head. 'Take that terrible jacket off and restore Bones' dignity.'

Anji knelt beside the dog. 'Actually, I think he likes it. He's a convert to glitz.'

Bones licked her fingers.

'So Tris is ready to go on and Dan is prepared to stay off: I guess that's what we call compromise.' Leo grinned.

Dan and Tris realized they'd been had.

'Get him!' said Tris. They both bundled on top of Leo and wrestled him to the floor.

'How shall we play this, Dan?' asked Tris, sitting on Leo's stomach.

'I don't mind. Whatever seems best to all of us.'

'Do we let him up?' Tris bounced once, making Leo suffer just a little more.

'I suppose we might as well – seeing how his plan worked out OK.'

'Great, because Anji and I have an idea.' Leo rolled out from under Tris and took out the song he and

Anji had co-written.

Tris scanned it quickly. 'To the same tune as 'Lost Bunny'?'

'Yes, with this chord change at the end. What do you think, Dan?'

He looked up from his sheet music. 'Go for it.'

'Bones?' asked Anji.

'He's OK as long as he gets a treat,' said Tris. He inspected his pink trousers. 'Oh boy. I wish I'd brought a change.'

Leo pulled out a pair of jeans and a black T-shirt. 'These do?'

'You are a lifesaver, Leo. Thanks.'

'What are friends for, hey?'

Dressed in matching jeans and black T-shirts, the four band members waited in the wings, sharing the space with several of the other acts who had already performed. An Irish boy band preened as they flirted with the make-up girls. A street dance crew hung out with the stagehands, trying to act as if they hadn't compromised their credibility by appearing on such a cheesy show. Out on the stage, the host, top TV comedian Jasper James, cracked jokes about the

baton-twirling majorettes who had just performed
a vigorous tap-dance. He was given the cue that the
band was finally ready to come on.

'And now, please raise the roof for our youngest
stars: The Cutie Pies and their Faithful Hound, Bows!'

The crowd hooted, whistled and applauded as
they walked on. Worried murmuring buzzed in the
studio as their change of appearance was noticed.
Leo went right up to the microphone.

'Hello, everyone. We are here tonight not as
The Cutie Pies but as four friends who messed up.

But we'd like to explain ourselves in our song. It's called 'Domino Effect'.' He picked up his guitar and ducked back to the mic. 'Oh and the dog's name is Bones – the kind you crunch, not the sort you tie.'

A ripple of laughter went round the room. That was good – it didn't sound as if they were going to be chased off the stage before they had a chance to set the record straight.

Leo glanced over at the judges. Not so good. Zane Jackson looked as though he would cheerfully murder them, incinerate their bodies, then scatter the ashes on the grave of The Cutie Pies.

Tris started the song with the drum introduction.

'*I took a step, reached for the prize,*' Leo sang,

'*Too many flaws destroy my disguise.*

I'm struggling – this isn't me.'

Anji played the guitar riff. Leo began to relax. This was so much better, no matter the outcome.

'*I lined them up so they could run,*

Flicked my finger, now it's begun.

I watch them fall – it's unstoppable.'

He took a step back to be in line with Anji and Dan as they joined him for the chorus.

'I can't pretend, I admit my defeat,
I can't do cute and I'm just not sweet.
Release the domino, the domino,
Release the domino effect.
I'm back to my sound, back to my sound.'

Leo knew he was saying goodbye to his chance of a contract and the fame that *Star Makers* promised, but it didn't matter. It felt really great to be singing with his friends, coming clean so they didn't have to carry on the pretence.

He could tell the others were enjoying it too: Anji was jigging about in her black skinny jeans and T-shirt, skull earrings dancing as she played her electric guitar. Tris was tapping the drums with his usual snarl and snap. Dan plucked the bass with his shy mastery of his instrument. Yeah, they were all back in their normal places, being themselves.

When they finished the crowd was silent for a few crucial seconds, then stood to applaud. Leo couldn't tell if it was for the confession or because they had genuinely liked the song. Now it was time for the judges' verdict.

The presenter glanced nervously over at them.

'That was, well ... unexpected,' he said. 'That was –
am I getting this right, guys – *not* The Cutie Pies?'

'I think you can just call us The Friends,' said Leo.

Dan put his arm around Anji and hugged her to
his side. If the judges were going to get tough with
them, it looked like Dan was ready to protect her
from the worst.

'So Zane – what did you think?' asked Jasper.

'I hated it. Boring, boring, boring – and did
I say, boring?'

The crowd started booing.

'I don't understand: they had such a strong image
going for them and they've thrown it away. They
are OK singers and performers but there's no longer
that special something. A big "No!" from me.' Zane
crossed his arms and glowered.

The audience didn't concur. Leo could see his mum
standing on her chair and shaking her fist at Zane.

Jasper patted Leo on the back. 'OK, Sadie, give us
your verdict. Try to be a bit kind, won't you – they
are our youngest performers and you are about to
crush their dreams.'

'Well now, I don't know about that.' Sadie was

sitting forward with an amused sparkle in her eyes. 'I have to say, I much prefer this version than the sugar overload of last week. You wrote that yourself?'

'Yes. Dan does our music; Anji and I write the lyrics,' said Leo. 'Tris holds us all together by keeping our feet on the ground.'

'And I guess you came down to earth with a bump last week. You really have something, you know, and I'd say that something is a special atmosphere between you. You call yourselves The Friends but I'd say you've made many more friends tonight with that song. We all make mistakes; not so many sing about it in front of millions.' The audience laughed. 'I think I can use that vibe, so that's a big "Yes!" from me.' She leant forward. 'Hi, Bones – love the tutu.'

Jasper swept his arms wide. 'There we have it, ladies and gentlemen: another split decision. But tonight it is *you* who will decide. The judges' marks are for guidance only. Vote for your favourite act and tune in for the results in an hour's time.'

The Friends exited the stage, greeted by smiles and nods from the backstage crew.

'Great performance, kids,' said the assistant.

'Reinventing yourself like that is good television.'

'Thanks, but that wasn't why ... ' Leo began, but Tris pulled him away.

'We don't want to spoil it now.'

'Spoil what?' asked Dan.

'Our chance of winning.' Tris shut the door to the dressing room and turned the key so no one could interrupt.

'You want to win?' Anji danced with Bones in her arms.

'If only to wipe the smile off Zane's face, then yeah.'

They passed the hour catching up with each other and telling jokes, trying not to think about all the phone calls pouring in from around the country. The knock on the door summoned them back to the stage. As they gathered with the other performers, they were pleased to find quite a few came up to them.

'Hated The Cutie Pies,' said one boy singer cheerfully, 'but like The Friends. Good luck!'

'And you,' said Leo.

'Oh, I don't stand much of a chance. Zane is now throwing his weight behind the tap-dancing majorettes. He wants a novelty act to win this year.

Still, it's all publicity for us, isn't it?'

'For us it's just fun.'

'Best attitude to have.'

'Let's bring our performers back on-stage,' called Jasper.

The Friends followed the singer on-stage but found they were jostled back by the twenty-strong troupe of tap-dancers in white uniforms who had been given prime position in the middle of the stage. They were pushed to join the street dance crew somewhere near the edge.

Dan shrugged. 'Guess that's it then.'

Bones nipped one of the tassels off the baton of the nearest majorette and began to chew it vengefully.

Tris grinned at him. 'You know something, Dan – I think being a tap-dancing majorette is possibly worse than being a Cutie Pie.'

'You think?' They both fell about laughing, totally ignoring the calls for silence.

'I have the results here. Remember, guys, all of you are winners to have got this far. So, third place goes to … (drum beats) … Johnny Kilkenny!'

The singer they had been talking to hurried to

the front of the stage, more surprised by his good
fortune than anyone.

'Oh wow, thanks!' He accepted his trophy and
moved to one side.

'And second place goes to ... (drums again) ... Tap
and Go!'

Screams from the majorettes as they mobbed
Jasper to receive their statuette. He emerged from
the crowd with twenty different lipstick marks on
his face.

'You don't think ... ?' asked Leo.

'Surely not,' said Dan.

Bones perked up his ears and stopped chewing on
the tassel.

'And now, the result you have all been waiting for: the winner of this year's *Star Makers* competition is ... (drums) ... I'm just opening the envelope (more drums) ... is the band once known as The Cuties Pies, now The Friends!'

Rapturous applause exploded from all sides. Leo saw his mum collapse in a swoon into Tris' dad's arms, quickly revived by a splash of cold tea from a flask provided by a friendly pensioner.

'We did it,' said Anji, too astonished to move.

'Come down the front, Cutie Friends, or whatever you're called these days, come get your prize!'

Bones led the way; Tris, Dan, Leo and Anji following behind in a daze. Leo found one of his hands being pumped up and down by the presenter and a contract was shoved in the other.

'I can see you are blown away by the news. And here come the judges to give you their own special congratulations.'

Zane swept by without so much as a nod.

'Very special,' said Jasper, winking at the camera.

Sadie shook each of them by the hand, or paw in Bones' case. 'Fabulous performance, kids. We start work next week on your single.' She patted Leo on the cheek as he stared at her in shock.

Then their friends and families were invited to join them on the stage. Their classmates edged the majorettes out of the way and formed an honour guard around the band. Dan's mum and dad shook hands with everyone in sight. Tris' dad lurked in a cool yet chuffed way at the back. Then Mum arrived.

'Oh no. The T-shirt!' moaned Anji.

She swept on-stage, crying, 'My babies!' and hugged them to her chest. At least that hid what was printed on the shirt.

'It's OK,' Leo told his sister as they surfaced from the hug. 'We can just tell everyone she's being ironic.'

'You rock, brother.'

'So do you, sister.'

They bumped knuckles and turned to join in the celebrations.

About the author

I am a multi-award-winning writer
for children and young adults. Before becoming
an author I worked as a British diplomat and
Oxfam policy adviser, but writing is definitely
the most fun! I have published over thirty books
in genres ranging from historical adventure to
fantasy. Over half a million of my books have
been sold worldwide in many languages.

I am a keen critic of talent shows and often
wonder where they get the awful acts, so I
decided to write a story to imagine how some
talented young singers might get themselves
caught up in the madness.